I Feel Relatively Neutral About New York

ALSO BY THE AUTHORS

I Could Go Either Way About Chicago

I'm Really Up in the Air About Portland

Los Angeles Certainly Has Its Pluses and Minuses

Austin, Huh? Yeah, Maybe. On the Other Hand, Maybe Not.

I Don't Want to Make a Fuss, but Sacramento?

Reno: Take It or Leave It

I 😐 NY

By Avery Monsen and Jory John

CHRONICLE BOOKS

SAN FRANCISCO

Image credits:

Corbis: © *Bettmann/CORBIS:* 49; **Myles Davidson** /stock.xchng: 75; **Jory John:** 83 top left; **Avery Monsen:** 15, 17, 25 left, 27, 33, 43, 47, 51 top, 55, 57, 63, 77; **Jim Naureckas:** 59; **Marielle Solan (www.MarielleSolan.com):** 31, 39, 40 bottom left, 83 bottom right; **Petteri Sulonen:** 87; **Veer:** © *Yuri Arcurs /Veer:* 51 bottom, © *Stephane Benito /Veer:* 73 (Earth), © *bernjuer /Veer:* 41 bottom, © *Cepn /Veer:* 40 top, © *Coprid /Veer:* 51 second from bottom, © *Corbis Photography /Veer:* 71, © *Cheryl Davis /Veer:* 83 bottom left, © *ErickN /Veer:* 13, © *Habman_18 /Veer:* 83 top right, © *kovalvs /Veer:* 65, © *Only Fabrizio /Veer:* 41 top, © *Pedro /Veer:* 51 second from top, © *pzAxe /Veer:* 21, © *Pere Sanz /Veer:* 73 (Space), © *Lee Snider /Veer:* 80, © *stu99 /Veer:* 35, © *Hieng Ling Tie /Veer:* 84–85, © *thatsmymop /Veer:* 25 right, © *Pakhnyushkhyy Vitaliy /Veer:* 75 (Money)

Library of Congress Cataloging-in-Publication Data is available.

ISBN: 978-0-8118-7456-4

Manufactured in China

Design and illustration by Avery Monsen and Jon Adams

10 9 8 7 6 5 4 3 2 1

Chronicle Books LLC
680 Second Street
San Francisco, California 94107
www.chroniclebooks.com

There is no place like [New York], no place with an atom of its glory, pride, and exultancy. It lays its hand upon a man's bowels; he grows drunk with ecstasy; he grows young and full of glory, he feels that he can never die.

—THOMAS WOLFE

If you're into that sort of thing.

—AVERY AND JORY

CONTENTS

Foreword by the Statue of Liberty 8

Introduction 10
Empire State Building 12
Statue of Liberty 14
Times Square 16
New York Pizza 18
FAO Schwarz 20
Ellis Island 22
Lincoln Center 24
American Museum of Natural History 26
Saturday Night Live 28
Katz's Delicatessen 30
The Subway 32
Grand Central Terminal 34
Strand Books 36
Ice Skating Rink at Rockefeller Center 38
Street Food 40
Apple Store 42
Chrysler Building 44
Taxis 46
Old-Timey Photos of Construction Workers Eating Lunch on Beams of
   Skyscrapers with No Harnesses or Anything 48
Central Park 50

Guggenheim Museum 52

Walking 54

Huge, Sometimes-Open Stairwells Right in the

   Middle of the Damn Sidewalk 56

Union Square 58

New York Newspapers 60

New York Public Library 62

Fashion Week 64

Greenwich Village. 66

The New Yorker 68

Snow 70

Sex and the City 72

Wall Street 74

United Nations 76

New York Bagels 78

Chinatown 80

Broadway 82

A Guide to the Public Restrooms of the City of New York 84

"The City That Never Sleeps" 86

Conclusion. 88

Appendix 90

About the Authors 94

I Feel Relatively Disappointed by This Book Hate-Mail Form 95

FOREWORD BY THE STATUE OF LIBERTY

Hello, huddled readers, and welcome to this book about New York. My name is Lady "Statue of" Liberty, and I live on a very small island off a very big island, called Manhattan. Heard of it?

I'm pretty famous. Not, like, *Angelina Jolie* famous, but famous enough where you've probably seen me on a postcard, or a TV show about New York, or a 3-D Magic Eye poster in a doctor's office. Some of you have even waited in line to enter me, which sounds like the premise for a dirty movie (!!!) ROFL!

Truth be told, sometimes it's hard to be a representation of life, liberty, and the pursuit of happiness, especially while keeping my arm in this position. *You* try holding a torch above your head for 120 years. Seriously, the other statues were going on and on about isometrics, and how keeping my arm up like this would build muscle . . . but then I started to think, "What's the point of building muscle when it's all in one green arm and I can't move?" Then I thought, "What's the point of *anything*?"

So here we are. And this foreword is supposed to be about New York, and about this book, and how I feel about both. Let's start with the book: When I heard the premise, about being neutral about New York, I laughed out loud, at least in my mind. I thought that was funny, especially since everybody's always going on and on about how great this place is. And *some* parts may be great, sure, but *you* try standing here, facing this brutal northbound wind and being gawked at by a bunch of mouth-breathers for decades on end. Does that sound fun to you?

And then there was that time that David Copperfield made me disappear. Let me tell you: That was some serious bullshit. Not only did he *not really* make me disappear (which would've been some sweet relief, let me tell you), but the whole time he was just prancing around with this wind machine delicately tousling his hair. A *wind machine*. LOL! We got plenty of the real thing here, Dave. Why don't you use a *pollution machine*, too? Or an *obnoxious tourists machine*? LMAO!

Now, a lot of people are probably like, "Lady 'Statue of' Liberty, what's your point?" My point is this: In my century-plus standing guard at the tippy-top, tuppy-tup of New York City, I've seen it all. The good, the bad, the ugly, the immigrants, the emigrants, the babies. I've seen the Yankees win the championship twenty-seven times, and the Knicks win eight conference titles, and I've seen Donald Trump turn this place into his personal ego trip. I've also seen the spirit of New York, when everybody has united, and I've seen the worst that the people and the city has to offer. Yes, I am a witness to it all.

Like many New Yorkers, I'm an outsider, originally from France, now living in the melting pot full-time and doing my best to thrive and survive. Like many New Yorkers, I was skeptical about this book at first, but then I started thinking about it and how it actually does a pretty good job summing up my feelings about the island of Manhattan and its surrounding boroughs, whether it's the pizza, buildings, bagels, or subway. I thought I'd be the last statue on Earth to say this, but I, too, feel relatively neutral about New York. And that's a fact.

In conclusion, please buy ten copies of this book. (I'm getting a percentage.)

Sincerely,

Lady Liberty ☺❀☮!!

Lady "Statue of" Liberty

INTRODUCTION

New York City. The Capital of the Free World. The Big Apple That Never Sleeps, Even When It's Asked Nicely. And so forth.

There are plenty of ways to argue that New York is the best city in the history of cities. Just ask anyone wearing an *I* ♥ *NY* T-shirt. They're easy to spot and they'll go on for at least twenty New York Minutes, which, in standard U.S. time, is about seventeen minutes and thirty-two seconds. (The conversion is complicated and depends on the position of Earth relative to the moon.)

But what about the rest of us, who think that at least sixteen of those New York Minutes might be nonsense? What about the hardworking, everyday folks who appreciate that, yes, New York is a pretty big city with a bunch of legitimately great things to offer, but it's also (hear us out) sort of a hassle? Yes, it's got amazing restaurants and tall buildings and important cultural events every night, but (again: please hear us out) there's just so much hustle and bustle! Over here: hustle! Over there: bustle! Over here: a small puddle of urine! Over there: still more bustle! And if New York is so great, how come everybody clears out during the summer months? Answer: because it's hot and uncomfortable. Ever smelled hot, uncomfortable urine? That's why.

Do we hate New York? No. Do we ♥ it? Occasionally. It depends. More often than not, we're somewhere in the middle. Relatively neutral, if you will. On a scale from one to *spectacular*, we generally give New York a five. And we think there are millions of people in countless cities, states, and commonwealths[1] that would agree.

---

1. We hope you'll cosign on this one, American Samoa. It's the least you can do.

All right. We know what you're thinking. You're all: *Why the eff would somebody write a book about New York, when they don't have any particularly strong feelings about it, one way or another?! And why the eff would we read that effing book?* To you, Aggressive Question Asker, we say: See? Exactly. Why so overheated, fella or lady-fella? And why are you waving that bagel at us so menacingly? Take it down a notch. Mellow out. Cool your New York Jets. When that's over with, cool your New York Mets, whatever that means.

(And for those of you who aren't feeling it, we've enclosed a handy *I Feel Relatively Disappointed by This Book* form on p. 95. Simply purchase a copy of this book, fill out the form, and send it to our publisher. If you really hate it, buy *two* copies, so you can send *two* letters. It's simple math.)

The deepest satisfactions in life come from enjoying something for exactly what it is, and not getting bent out of shape over what it isn't, or what you want it to be. New York is a lot of things, but it might not actually be what everyone makes it out to be. Right? Consider this book a guide to getting the most out of, and being the least disappointed in, your relationship with New York, whether you live there or not.

So come along, why don't you, on our ill-conceived, minimally researched journey through the Empire City. We can't promise you'll have fun, but we can promise it'll only be ninety-six pages, and a lot of those pages are pictures.

Shrug? Shrug, indeed.

EMPIRE STATE BUILDING

Have you ever stood atop the Empire State Building—the absolute highest point on Earth—gazing across all of Manhattan in the fading sunlight, pondering what brought you here and where you're going, realizing that this is probably the closest you'll ever be to heaven? Have you ever done that? Neither have we.

But we do have to admit that it's really neat that this is the tallest building in the world. Really. The tallest in the world? That's a big deal. You put your mind on something and you *nailed* it, New York. Absolutely nailed it. And ain't nobody taking that away from you. Congratulations on this. So let's just move on to the next . . .

What's that?

It's not the *what*? Not the tallest *anything*? So, wait . . . when was it beaten . . . in 1954? By the Griffin Television Tower, in *Oklahoma*? So, you're saying that New York has had a relatively tall building for the last fifty years? Huh.

This. Is. Awkward.

Okay. Tell you what: The Empire State Building definitely *seems* to be taller than everything in its general vicinity. So as long as nobody's putting up any super-tall Starbucks[1] or giant Walgreens on 5th Avenue anytime soon, your secret's safe with us, E. S. Building.

> **PROS:** Very tall. Crazy tall. Almost too tall.
> **CONS:** Not tall enough.
> **CONCLUSION:** (Uncomfortable smile)

---

1. *Possible name: "The Venti Building."*

AS OF PRESS TIME, THE SIXTEENTH TALLEST FREE-STANDING STRUCTURE IN THE WORLD.
THAT'S FAIRLY TALL!

STATUE OF LIBERTY

Lady Liberty. The Old Maid of the Sea. Old Green Eyes. Created in 1492,[1] this statue gives all kinds of hope to the huddled masses, and it's probably the biggest liberty-related statue you'll encounter. So that's good. That's very good, and we all need to be inspired from time to time. And hey, a torch-bearing 150-foot French broad really does it for some people.[2]

On the other hand, wasn't it just a little bit satisfying to see Ms. Liberty up and disappear at the creepy-yet-delicate hands of David Copperfield? Or to see that big, pointy head roll in *Cloverfield*? Because, sure, the statue is a symbol of freedom and openness and the American dream, but it's just as much a symbol of sweaty tourists elbowing you out of the way for a snapshot of their dumb kids pretending to hold the torch.

And just how majestic is it to see seagulls pooping all over the physical manifestation of Liberty, all day, every day?

Answer: It's only sort of majestic.

> **PROS:** Awe-inspiring symbol of hope and possibility.
> **CONS:** Honestly, it kind of smells.
> **CONCLUSION:** We'll think about it.

1. Or something. Our next book: I Feel Relatively Neutral About Research.
2. 150-foot Frenchmen.

CONTAINED WITHIN THE STATUE OF LIBERTY

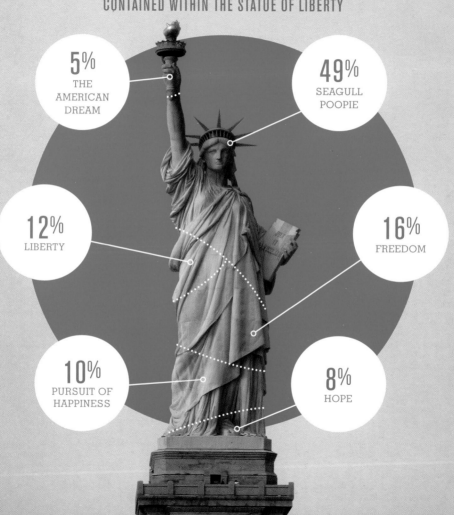

5% THE AMERICAN DREAM

49% SEAGULL POOPIE

12% LIBERTY

16% FREEDOM

10% PURSUIT OF HAPPINESS

8% HOPE

TIMES SQUARE

Ah, Times Square, the Crossroads of the World, home to various ball droppings and Naked Cowboys.[1]

You're a major intersection of commerce, Times Square, what with your Bubba Gumps and your Planet Hollywoods and a lot of other quaint mom-and-pop shops, including Bubba Hollywoods and Planets Gump.

And you've certainly cleaned up your seediness, as of late, replacing porno theaters with Disney stores and replacing homeless squeegee guys with Disney stores.[3] Great job on that.

Unfortunately, with all your Jumbotrons and blinky news crawlers, we can't think straight. We try, but just as we're about to think straight, an animated super-sign *razzle-dazzles* that notion right out of our heads, and suddenly we've got an uncontrollable urge to put on some mouse ears and buy a Samsung phone while drinking a Coke. And, sure, overwhelming comes with the flashy, glitzy territory. But, seriously, if we wanted a seizure, we'd induce it ourselves. Whatever that means.

> **PROS:** Razzle-dazzle, hubbub.
> **CONS:** Seizures, Naked Cowboys.
> **CONCLUSION:** Rain check?

1. *And, unfortunately, the Naked Cowboy's balls dropping.[2]*
2. *Gross. Sorry . . .*
3. *Hot seller: toy squeegees!*

HERE'S A NEWS CRAWLER FOR YOU, TIMES SQUARE:
YOU ARE OVERWHELMING . . . YOU ARE OVERWHELMING . . . YOU ARE OVERWHELMING . . .

NEW YORK PIZZA

God, we love New York pizza. Yum yum yummers. Yummity yim yams.

Right? Of course. But now that we're thinking about it, you know what New York pizza reminds us of? It reminds us of every pizza, everywhere. Tampa pizza. Des Moines pizza. Albuquerque pizza. You know why? As it turns out, pizza is just cheese and sauce on top of bread.

We know what you're thinking: "No, it's not."

But our point is: "Yes, it is. It absolutely is."

And we can prove it. With science. And cheese. And sauce. And more science. And some bread.

Here's our experiment: Give us a blindfold, a slice of cheese pizza from Brooklyn, and another from Guam. You honestly won't know the difference. Honestly.

Case closed. If you don't believe that, you don't believe in science.

> **PROS:** All pizza, everywhere, is really, really delicious. Yim yum.
> **CONS:** New York pizza is just pizza. And it's going straight to your hips.
> **CONCLUSION:** (Half-shrug)

CAN YOU MATCH EACH PIZZA SLICE WITH ITS PLACE OF ORIGIN?

1

A NEW YORK CITY

2

B BOSTON

3

C SAN FRANCISCO

4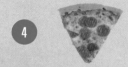

D SEATTLE

5

E GUAM

ANSWER: NO. NO, YOU CAN'T.

FAO SCHWARZ

Do you remember when, in fourth grade, your friend Chris Havermeyer came back from winter vacation, having visited his grandparents on the East Coast? He could barely contain himself. "They've got the biggest toy store in the world," he whispered, his eyes filling with tears of joy. "It's everything we ever wanted."

And then you watched *Big* and the legend grew. Any old toy store would have drawn you in; your tiny, idiotic child-brain always went fuzzy for anything new and shiny and plastic. But this was the mother of all toy stores, the closest thing to Santa's workshop you were ever going to encounter. You swore that one day you'd make it to this shining mecca. You'd pound out "Chopsticks" on that giant piano and take home a huge stuffed elephant if it was your last worldly act.

Now, of course, you're an adult, and you realize upon entering FAO Schwarz that this is just a toy store. These toys aren't made in Santa's workshop. They're made in China, where the toys are made by elves, if by "elves" you mean "children." And the *Big* piano has since been replaced with a look-alike and pushed off into a corner. And what were you thinking buying that stuffed elephant? There's no way that's fitting in your tiny apartment, unless you move the bed next to the sink and the bookshelf into the bathroom in what will seem like the largest, saddest game of Tetris ever played.

On the door, at adult eye level, they should inscribe, "Abandon hope, all ye who enter here," because that, my friends, is the death of a dream.

> **PROS:** It's a very large toy store.
> **CONS:** Chris Havermeyer has given you unreasonable expectations of what a very large toy store can be.
> **CONCLUSION:** If you need a toy, they might have it. If you're chasing a dream, probably better just to rent *Big*.

SEEMED LIKE A GOOD IDEA AT THE TIME

This used to be $74.50 in your pocket. Now it's one step closer to your appearance on *Hoarders*. It's time to find Chris Havermeyer on Facebook and tell him off.

ELLIS ISLAND

It was the gateway to our great nation, where some twelve million immigrants took their first steps out of cramped, disease-filled freighters, in search of the American Dream.[1] Now, of course, to get there, you can just take a cramped, disease-filled ferry, which leaves every thirty minutes from Battery Park. To get on the ferry, you have to go through an elaborate screening process, removing belts and shoes and jackets. It feels almost like the Ellis Island of the 1800s, but with fewer filthy Irish![2]

On the island, you can take hourly ranger-guided tours (semi-interesting) or look up your genealogy in the museum's American Family Immigration History Center (semi-boring[3]).

Sure, Ellis Island's an important part of history. But it turns out you can look up all that ancestry stuff online. (Plus watch hilarious cat videos!) And on the Internet, there's little to no chance you'll miss the last ferry off the island and be trapped overnight, subject to the ghostly nagging of your immigrant ancestors about why you never call.

> **PROS:** History.
> **CONS:** History can be sort of a hassle.
> **CONCLUSION:** If you've got nothing better to do, maybe.

1. *A sixty-inch TV and a four-pound bag of Doritos.*
2. *Just kidding, Irish. Nothing but love.*
3. *Just kidding, family. Nothing but love.*

SHOULD YOU VISIT ELLIS ISLAND?

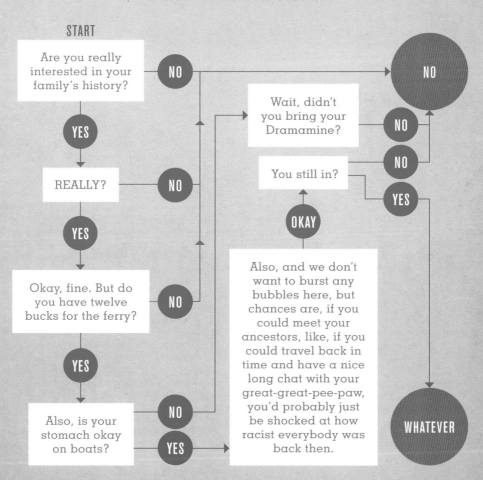

LINCOLN CENTER

Just like Abraham Lincoln himself, Lincoln Center is ten stories tall and gorgeous. When you walk up to the center on a cold, starry night and you gaze into his dreamy eyes . . . er, through its dreamy windows at the swirly Marc Chagall angel murals hanging within, you can't help thinking that President Lincoln, upon looking inside, would marvel at its grandeur. And then he'd probably wonder how he had been transported 150 years into the future. He'd see you using your cell phone. But then, because he's Abraham Lincoln, he'd probably figure it out. Did you know he patented a system to alter the buoyancy of steamboats? It's true. He was like his era's Ron Popeil, inventor of the Showtime Rotisserie, Chop-O-Matic, Veg-O-Matic, Smokeless Ashtray, and the Cap Snaffler, which snaffles caps off any size jug, bottle, or jar. Did Lincoln have caps in need of snaffling? We'll never know.

But that's neither here nor there.

Inside Lincoln Center, miles of red carpet will make you feel like television's Joan Rivers,[1] and the center's rich and dynamic programs featuring the philharmonic orchestra, ballet, symphony, opera, chamber music, jazz, theater arts, and avant-garde films can make you feel uniquely and efficiently uncultured when you walk past it to go see the latest 3-D *Jackass* movie at the AMC 13 multiplex three blocks up.

> **PROS:** Named after Lincoln.
> **CONS:** Would probably frighten Lincoln.
> **CONCLUSION:** You're probably underdressed.

---

1. Or, to an equally grating extent, television's Melissa Rivers.

LINCOLN THE CENTER VS. LINCOLN THE MAN

Sixteen acres

A complex of buildings

Home to twelve major performance facilities

Accepts five-dollar bills and pennies (among other money)

Free music on Thursdays

Sixteenth president of our nation

A complex individual

Home to 206 bones, 600 muscles, and 22 major internal organs

Pictured on five-dollar bills and pennies (among other memorabilia)

Freed the slaves, forever

SLIGHT ADVANTAGE: LINCOLN THE MAN

AMERICAN MUSEUM OF NATURAL HISTORY

We stood in the lobby for a while. It's a pretty nice space, with a giant dinosaur skeleton in the middle. We were tempted to touch it—it's so lifelike!—but there were four security guards eyeing us. Security guards ruin everything. Don't even get us started on our blocked attempt to get inside Trump Tower, for purposes of research. That was some serious bullshit. Who does this Trump guy think he is?

Anyway, there's an important distinction between the museum's lobby and the rest of the building. The lobby is free, whereas you have to pay a "suggested donation" to see everything else. We don't respond well to "museum guilt," or "supporting the arts," so we simply sat and watched the dinosaur. Nothing much happened. Granted, it was nice that some archaeologists took the time to piece this guy together and all, and to pose him in a lifelike fashion, but honestly, it was kind of a letdown. Turns out, if you've seen one huge dinosaur skeleton, you've kind of seen them all.

The takeaway? Not nearly as many exhibits come to life as *Night at the Museum* would have you believe.

> **PROS:** Dinosaur bones, precious jewels, planetarium.
> **CONS:** Ben Stiller is a liar.
> **CONCLUSION:** Whatever.

NATURE

THERE IS A DELIGHT IN THE
HARDY LIFE OF THE OPEN

THERE ARE NO WORDS THAT CAN
TELL THE HIDDEN SPIRIT OF THE
WILDERNESS THAT CAN REVEAL
ITS MYSTERY, ITS MELANCHOLY
AND ITS CHARM

THE NATION BEHAVES WELL IF IT
TREATS THE NATURAL RESOURCES
AS ASSETS WHICH IT MUST TURN
OVER TO THE NEXT GENERATION
INCREASED AND NOT IMPAIRED
IN VALUE

CONSERVATION MEANS DEVELOPMENT
AS MUCH AS IT DOES PROTECTION

"ALL MY FRIENDS ARE DEAD."

SATURDAY NIGHT LIVE

There's no denying that *Saturday Night Live* is a cultural institution. Seriously, don't try.

But hey! You know when everybody's always all, "You can't *touch* those early days of *SNL*," and you're all like, "Yeah, everything used to be so brilliant and laugh-out-loud funny. It's a cultural institution!" And then your friend Dave walks into the room, and he's all like, "Did I hear you guys talking about my favorite institution of culture: early *SNL*? It is untouchable. Like that one vase on your top shelf, Marta." And then Marta's all, "Um, that's an urn." And then everybody's silent for a while, including the urn.

But here's something weird: Have you seen early *SNL* recently? Take a look. For every solid laugh, there are two or three or thirteen sketches that just end with a coked-up Chevy Chase bumbling his lines and taking a spill and permanently injuring his back. Nostalgia has its place, sure.[1] But let's call it like it is and say the show's always had its ups and downs.

We'll keep watching, yes, but only because it's on.

> **PROS:** Bill Murray, Eddie Murphy, Phil Hartman, Amy Poehler.
> **CONS:** Joe Piscopo, Chris Kattan, Molly Shannon, Cheri Oteri.
> **CONCLUSION:** Pretty okay.

---

1. *Nostalgiaville, which is an actual city in Ohio!*[2]
2. *Not an actual city.*

LAUGHTER BY YEAR: 1975 TO PRESENT

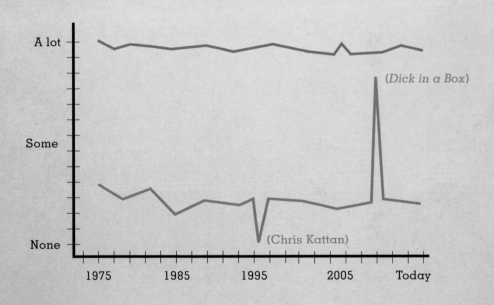

A lot

Some

None

(Dick in a Box)

(Chris Kattan)

1975   1985   1995   2005   Today

KEY

SNL

Tickling

KATZ'S DELICATESSEN

Katz's Deli: Meg Ryan totally faked an orgasm in there, and it was totally in a movie. So if you're the type of person who likes to eat in places where famous people fake orgasms, then we wholeheartedly recommend Katz's.

However, if you don't know whether you're that type of person, we've got a quick quiz to help you decide. Which of the following best completes this sentence: "I'm hungry, and I'd like a sandwich, "

_____

A) . . . so let's go to whatever deli is closest and tastiest.

B) . . . so let's go where the service is passable and the facilities are reasonably well maintained and hygienic.

C) . . . but what I really want to know is, did Meg Ryan, at some point, pretend to have an orgasm at our proposed dining establishment? That's really all I'm looking for. Sandwiches are good, too, I guess, as long as when I get there I can point at a woman and say, "I'll have what she's having," and everybody will burst into spontaneous laughter and/or applause and/or orgasm.

If you chose A or B, you might want to consider any number of relatively decent dining establishments in the area. But if you chose C, congratulations! Katz's is your destination. Enjoy your eighteen-dollar sandwich. It'll be worth every penny! Probably!

> **PROS:** Delicious, hand-carved pastrami, with a side of celebrity 'gasm.
> **CONS:** Every sandwich looks like a pig exploded into some bread.
> **CONCLUSION:** Eat what you want. It's your life.

KATZ'S PRICE BREAKDOWN

5¢
BREAD

2¢
MUSTARD

75¢
PASTRAMI

$17
FAMOUS
FAKE
ORGASM

8¢
SAUERKRAUT

10¢
CHEESE

THE SUBWAY

Q. Where does it go?
A. Everywhere!

Q. How much does it cost?
A. Relatively little!

Q. What's that smell?
A. Urine!

> **PROS:** It can get you anywhere for only two dollars. Honestly, that is a totally reasonable amount of money to pay to get all over the place. Neat.
> **CONS:** We saw a rat on an L train. In the actual train car. We think it may have been going to work. Where did this particular rat work, you ask? On the J train.
> **CONCLUSION:** It's got problems, but we still use it.

POP QUIZ: WHICH DOOR DO YOU CHOOSE?

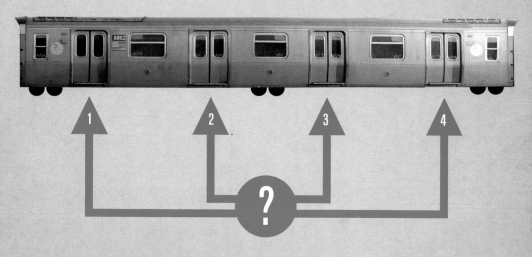

DOOR 1: Sit next to television's Alec Baldwin!

DOOR 2: Is that a small puddle of blood on the floor?

DOOR 3: A team of break-dancing teens performs
and asks you for money. One dancer seems
like his heart isn't really in it.

DOOR 4: Sit next to television's Stephen Baldwin! (He
also asks you for money.)

ANSWER: THERE IS NO RIGHT ANSWER. NAMASTE.

GRAND CENTRAL TERMINAL

Don't call it Grand Central *Station*. Whooo, buddy. Don't do that.

When it opened in 1871, it was called Grand Central *Depot*. Then they rebuilt it and called it a *station*. Then, in 1913, they rebuilt it again, and called it a *terminal*. That's what your cabbie will tell you if you call it Grand Central *Station*.

"It's a *terminal*!" he'll say, wrenching his body around to look you straight in the eyes. His name will be Tony, and he'll really know his stuff. "Did you know they recently filmed part of *Old Dogs* there?" he'll ask. You won't know that because you won't have seen *Old Dogs*. Nobody saw *Old Dogs*.

Then, about three minutes into Tony's impromptu Grand Central/*Old Dogs* lesson, you'll realize that, with his eyes on you and your eyes on him, there are quite literally *no eyes on the road*. Do the math! Not a single eye!

Well, don't worry. You'll make it to Grand Central Terminal. Tony's a pro! And you'll sit on the steps in the main concourse, with the vaulted ceilings and the huge clock, and you'll watch everyone rushing around to get to wherever they're going, and the light will stream in through those huge windows, and you'll feel like, yes, someone did something *very* right here.

And then a security guard will tell you not to sit on the steps. Because, at the end of the day, Grand Central Terminal doesn't care about your moments of clarity. It doesn't care that you've just found a little bit of peace within this crazy city. It's just a big train station, er, depot, er, *terminal*. Dang.

> **PROS:** It's a really nice place to almost have a really nice moment.
> **CONS:** As it turns out, there's a reason nobody saw *Old Dogs*.
> **CONCLUSION:** One thumb up.

THREE PEOPLE PICTURED HERE HAVE SEEN *OLD DOGS*. ONE ENJOYED IT.
HIS NAME: JOHN TRAVOLTA.

STRAND BOOKS

Oh, Strand, you boastful boaster. Yes, we're impressed. You have eighteen miles of books, and that certainly seems like more book-miles than most other people have. In the having-the-most-miles-of-books competition, you're the winner by a landslide, or a bookslide, which, *yikes*, we'd rather not think about while browsing your overstacked aisles.

At the same time, Strand, it should be noted that your building is not eighteen miles long. That would be crazy. It would stretch from Union Square in Manhattan to a *shark's den* in the *Atlantic Ocean*. And can you imagine books in the ocean? They'd get all wet. And there would be *sharks*!

Instead, those eighteen miles are folded over on top of each other in one tall building, like small intestines packed inside a torso, if intestines were organized by genre.[1] The books are all stacked up super-high, where nobody can reach them, and crammed into every little corner, where only the smallest among us could survive. By our estimate, twelve of those book-miles are too high to reach, and the other six miles are teen vampire romances. And who needs that many of those? Not us, Strand. Not us.

> **PROS:** Lots of books. Books everywhere.
> **CONS:** We're afraid they're going to fall on us.
> **CONCLUSION:** It would actually be a little more interesting as an eighteen-mile-long underwater reading room.

1. *Fun fact: Did you know that if you pulled your small intestine out and laid it in a straight line, it would be exactly eighteen miles long, just like Strand Books? It's true![2] If you laid it all out, it'd stretch all the way to a shark's den, where a family of sharks would quickly devour it. You'd be all, "Whoa, sharks, cut that out! I just wanted to see how far my small intestine would stretch if I laid it out in a straight line. Just because something reaches to your fucking shark's den doesn't mean there's an open invitation to chomp the hell out of it." But if we've learned anything from Shark Week, it's that, where small intestines are concerned, sharks just don't listen to reason.*
2. *Not actually true.*

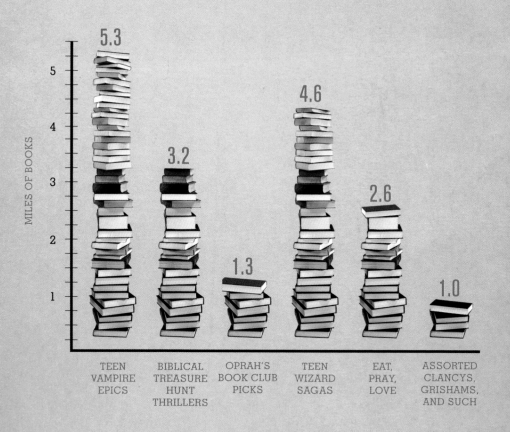

EIGHTEEN MILES OF BOOKS, BY THE NUMBERS

MILES OF BOOKS

5.3 — TEEN VAMPIRE EPICS
3.2 — BIBLICAL TREASURE HUNT THRILLERS
1.3 — OPRAH'S BOOK CLUB PICKS
4.6 — TEEN WIZARD SAGAS
2.6 — EAT, PRAY, LOVE
1.0 — ASSORTED CLANCYS, GRISHAMS, AND SUCH

IT ADDS UP TO EIGHTEEN MILES. WE CHECKED.

ICE SKATING RINK AT ROCKEFELLER CENTER

Like a United Nations on ice, the skating rink at Rockefeller Center is lined by flags representing all the nations of the world. At last, an ice rink where diplomats can wear Spandex and hold hands during couple's skate!

But somehow we weren't surprised to see three guys in the middle of the rink, skating around like they owned the place. These grandstanders—representing the People's Republic of Showoffistan—were twirling and leaping and lutzing and . . . is it clear that we don't know ice skating terminology?

Is a lutz even a thing?

In a way, it was kind of comforting to walk up to the rink and know—just *know*—that there would be three guys in the dead center, guys who have come out to the rink just about every day of their adult lives and who take it *so* seriously even though, to be totally blunt, all that lutzing probably isn't going to lead anywhere outside of this particular rink unless it ends up in the background of an Al Roker weather segment, before he tells you what's happening in *your* neck of the woods.

Today's forecast: three men, humbly dedicated to the beautiful art of ice dancing, with a slight chance of pent-up aggression and broken dreams. Sigh.

> **PROS:** The flags look neat and there's that big gold statue. That thing probably has a name.
> **CONS:** After about thirty seconds, you can't get away from the creeping thought that your entire life, every worldly choice you've made, has lead you to an ice skating rink.
> **CONCLUSION:** Brrrrr.

THE MOVES OF THE ICE RINK SHOWOFF

THE CRY FOR HELP

THE SHOWER SOB

THE SILENT SCREAM

THE DOUBLE-TWISTING
ABSENT FATHER

THE FULL-ROTATING
ONLY-RAMEN-EATER

STREET FOOD

HOT DOGS

Mmm: They're as American as an apple pie!

Hmm: (Apple pie made of reconstituted meat slurry, left in an all-day, dirty-water soak served by employees with no "must wash hands" policy.)

. . . .

NUTS 4 NUTS

Mmm: Roasted almonds and a sweet, crunchy coating are the Lennon & McCartney of the snack world. The Lennon-almond provides a solid, thoughtful core, while the ostentatious but skillful McCartney-coating sweetens the deal. Delicious.

Hmm: Maybe this is a matter of personal preference, but is anyone really taking those cashews seriously? The cashew is definitely Ringo. (The quiet, spiritual nut-bag is George.)

HALAL CART

Mmm: Gyros, kebabs, and chicken-and-rice plates! Have we died and gone to *heaven*? (In this afterlife scenario, lambs and chickens have also died and entered heaven, only to be immediately double-killed by butcher-angels and served to us as a tasty snack.)

Hmm: Make sure wherever you're going next has a comfortable bathroom. That's a lot of trust to put in a stranger with a metal box full of meat.

PRETZELS

Mmm: Totally filling! Totally inexpensive! Totally pretzels!

Hmm: It's like biting into a live python made entirely of carbohydrates. You'll enjoy the first two bites, before being hit in the kisser with a case of Ultimate Drymouth.

APPLE STORE

Okay, we're aware that there are other Apple Stores in other cities, but the 5th Avenue Manhattan location is so distinctive that we've given it its very own entry in our very own book. Why? Because this Apple Store is one big glassy box with a glass elevator in the middle and a see-through stairway, complete with wrap-around glass banister. If that wasn't enough, 90 percent of the *employees* are made out of glass. It's crazy that Apple management was somehow able to find so many recent college graduates whose bodies are made out of pure, hand-blown glass. We haven't seen so much glass, in fact, since the last time we were admiring our collection of early 1900s figurines shaped like fairies and baseball players, which sit on the shelf directly above our depressing spoon collection. And right below our *awesome* snow globe collection.

The 5th Avenue location is a temple in celebration of Apple's use of technology to demonstrate just how many greasy fingerprints you can leave on a smooth surface in the course of a day. When we were there, a lone, nontransparent Apple employee made a continual round of the cube to wipe off customers' smudgy fingerprints with his rag.[1]

Apple chose New York in which to place its crystal castle. Their message: New Yorkers enjoy high design. Our message: Jeez, New Yorkers, wash your hands!

> **PROS:** See-through building.
> **CONS:** Recognition that humans are inherently greasy.
> **CONCLUSION:** Think different? Think Dial Antibacterial Hand Soap.

---

1. *Granted, this was an iRag, which can communicate with other rags wirelessly.*

SERIOUSLY, PEOPLE. WASH UP. THERE'S NO APP FOR BETTER HYGIENE.

CHRYSLER BUILDING

True story: When William Van Alen was commissioned to design the Chrysler Building in the late 1920s, his only instruction was to make it the tallest building in the world. Turns out, the folks at the Bank of Manhattan commissioned Alen's former partner and contemporary rival, H. Craig Severance, to do the same thing at 40 Wall Street.[1] Thus, an unofficial tallest-building contest had begun. As far as we know, the winner would receive a gift card to Bed, Bath, and Beyond![2]

After going back and forth, changing their blueprints to make the buildings higher and better, Severance was sure that he'd won. "Ohmygosh, you guys, I think I, like, *won*," he gushed. But after the construction of 40 Wall Street was complete, Alen pulled out a secret weapon: a 123-foot-tall steel spire he'd been hiding in an elevator shaft. He won the contest by 121 feet. Check and mate, Severance.

Unfortunately, they were both beaten months later by the Empire State Building.

Unfortunately, the Empire State Building was beaten in 1954 by the Griffin Television Tower in Oklahoma.

Unfortunately, the Griffin Tower was beaten in 1956 by the KOBR-TV Tower in New Mexico.

And so forth. Moral? You should never try anything because you'll never be the best.

> **PROS:** It's very pretty.
> **CONS:** A monument to being the thirty-ninth best/tallest building.
> **CONCLUSION:** A for effort?

1. *Home of Tina Fey's little-known sitcom, 40 Wall.*
2. *Apparently, W. Van Alen really liked Memory Foam.*

SOME FAIRLY TALL THINGS

BURJ KHALIFA
2,717 ft

101 TAIPEI
1,667 ft

SWFC
1,614 ft

CHRYSLER
BUILDING
1,046 ft

KAREEM ABDUL-
JABAR STANDING ON
SHAQUILLE O'NEAL'S
SHOULDERS
14 ft

TAXIS

Some time ago, New Yorkers got together and decided they'd simply prefer to leave the driving to others.

"We'd rather not drive," they declaimed in unison with their New York accents. "We'd prefer to leave the driving to others. Also, the parking."

And so they did.

And cabs are pretty great because, let's face it: Owning a car can be sort of a drag. You have to worry about *tickets*, and *parking*, and at some point you'll probably be driving with some friends and you'll accidentally hit and kill a local fisherman. You'll dump his body in the ocean and make a blood pact with your friends never to speak of it again, but, *of course*, he'll come back and try to murder you with a hook.

Luckily, there are cabs everywhere in New York. Look at all those cabs! Tons of cabs! Almost *too many* cabs! So many, in fact, that it seems like they constitute 90 percent of the vehicles in any given New York traffic jam. Any given frustrating, inconvenient New York traffic jam. Hmm.

> **PROS:** There are literally a trillion cabs.
> **CONS:** There are literally a trillion cabs, bumper-to-bumper, between you and where you're trying to go.
> **CONCLUSION:** We can walk it from here.

CABS BY THE NUMBERS

Cabs speeding past you when you're just trying to cross the road.

Cabs around when you need one and it's late and raining and you're in sort of a bad neighborhood.

OLD-TIMEY PHOTOS OF CONSTRUCTION WORKERS EATING LUNCH ON BEAMS OF SKYSCRAPERS WITH NO HARNESSES OR ANYTHING

Guys: You're living in a time when New York is expanding up into the skies and it seems like anything is possible, and if you feel like eating your tuna fish sandwich on the exposed beam of a highrise, ain't nobody gonna hold you back. Okay. We get it.

Could you put on just a small harness, though? A wee little safety cable? Or put a net underneath you? Okay, sure, we understand how harnesses can chafe, but we imagine nets aren't too expensive in 1932, or whenever you are. We're getting heart palpitations just looking at you, and we're eighty years in the future. Our hands are clammy and our tongues are dry. Please be careful, Construction Workers Eating Lunch on Beams of Skyscrapers With No Harnesses or Anything. Think of your children.

And suppose you do, against all odds, manage to stay on that little beam. If your tuna sandy slips, there's going to be an old-timey gentleman below with your lunch permanently embedded into his forehead. Johnny Sandwich-Face, they'll call him. He'll have to go get a job in the sideshow at Coney Island, and *nobody* wants *that*.

> **PROS:** Your picture will be printed on posters in dorm rooms and offices, forever.
> **CONS:** You're making your mothers very upset.
> **CONCLUSION:** We'll stick with a poster of a puppy wearing sunglasses, trying to do a pull-up, thank you very much.

OUR HUMBLE SUGGESTIONS FOR ALL BRAVE MEN IN OLD-TIMEY PHOTOS:
1. HARNESS 2. NORSE FLYING HELMET 3. GYROCOPTER 4. *WINGARDIUM LEVIOSA* 5. NET

CENTRAL PARK

Central Park wasn't always the 843-acre Eden we know and love today. It was just a big, desolate swamp until the state decided to turn this wasteland into a wonderland, open to the rich and the poor, the cranky and the crankier. Designers Fredrick Law Olmsted and Calvert Vaux (actual names!), crafted the landscape meticulously, all to encourage New Yorkers to mingle, relax, get high, and play intramural sports with their shirts off.

So they hauled 1,444,800 cubic yards of earth, excavated 198,000 cubic yards of rock, and laid 95 miles of pipe below the park's surface to build and maintain the beautiful-but-artificial ponds. That's a lot of pipe![1]

Finally, in 1876, the park opened its gates. It was magnificent, and Olmsted and Vaux celebrated by smoking some pot and playing a shirts-and-skins kickball game with Ulysses S. Grant.[3]

But that was then and this is now. Central Park has gotten a bit of a bad rap over the last 130+ years, mostly due to how many bodies they find there in *Law & Order: SVU*. But the truth is that Central Park is a lovely and generally safe place to hang out, and we applaud those early pipe-layers for their forethought in preserving a little space on the island that wasn't covered in buildings. Granted, even Central Park has concrete and roads, but what are you going to do, complain? Don't be like us. It gets old after a while.

> **PROS:** Nature's great.
> **CONS:** Cars driving though it: kind of a bummer.
> **CONCLUSION:** It's really nice, but comparing it to actual nature is like comparing a sour apple Now and Later to an *actual* sour apple.

1. That's what she said.[2]
2. Sorry.
3. Our next book: I Feel Relatively Neutral About Historical Fiction.

THINGS TO DO IN CENTRAL PARK

Take a romantic horse-drawn carriage ride: We shelled out fifty bucks for one, and boy did *that* get uncomfortable. As it turns out, there's no easy way to convince a carriage-buggy driver that you're just two dudes trying to enjoy an ironic romantic carriage ride through Central Park.

Visit the Central Park Zoo: Depending on the time of year that you visit, it may look more like the Central Park Empty Cages.

Go ice skating: Central Park has a bigger rink than Rockefeller Center, but it can be just as crowded, so keep your eyes open for other skaters barreling toward you with the speed of Apolo Ohno and the grace of Yoko Ono.

Jog around like you own the place: You'll feel just like Dustin Hoffman in *Marathon Man*. But without all that Nazi torture. Hopefully!

GUGGENHEIM MUSEUM

Much like the Arby's in Elko, Nevada, the Guggenheim Museum is a Frank Lloyd Wright masterpiece. With its famous cylinder-and-slab construction and its great sloping interior ramp and rotunda, it's totally a signature of twentieth-century architecture.

Inside the museum, there are some six thousand works of art, which is sort of like storing art in art!

Our question: Do you think any of those artworks could possibly be used to hold other, *smaller* artworks inside them, to make some kind of art-in-art-in-art *turducken*? We don't think we're asking too much here, to demand that all sculptures contain paintings, and all paintings contain video installations, and all video installations feature tiny, mouse-size Claes Oldenburg hamburger-beanbag-chairs, smaller and smaller, into infinity. C'mon, Guggenheim! Get on it!

> **PROS:** Art is great, if you're into that sort of thing.
> **CONS:** Let's be honest: You're not. You haven't been passionate about anything in quite a while. You're depressed.
> **CONCLUSION:** Frank Lloyd Wright? More like Frank Lloyd *Wrong*. Zing!

Now imagine, if you will, that this artist's rendering is inside *another* artist's rendering. And the artist who created it—without getting too graphic— is literally *inside* another artist. Pretty wild stuff, huh? Yeah. Wild.

WALKING

There's nothing quite like the beautiful, surging chaos of the sidewalks of New York. It's a sea of humanity out there, in the summer a literal melting pot, where thousands of people with thousands of wants and dreams and flu-bugs and bedbugs converge to add up to something greater than any one of them.[1]

But like the treacherous undercurrent of the sea, the sidewalks of New York have their own potentially dangerous—or at the very least annoying—flow. Top scientists attribute this to the fact that New Yorkers seem to walk faster than anyone else in the world. Why are they going so fast? Where are they all going? Why don't they leave a few minutes earlier? We tried to ask, but everyone rushed right by us.

This fast-walking is especially hazardous around revolving doors, which are great at keeping out the drafts and noise of the streets,[2] but, coupled with the speed at which New Yorkers walk, also have the potential to spin like the frenzied blades of a food processor. Watch out, New Yorkers!

The point is, walking in New York can be a blessing and a curse. It's nice to live in a city where physical activity and fresh air are part of the daily routine (are you listening, Los Angeles?), but also, with all that walking, your feet are going to *kill* for the first few months.

> **PROS:** Self-reliance.
> **CONS:** Blisters.
> **CONCLUSION:** Jury's out.

---

1. *A several-thousand-legged, super-wanty-dreamy people-bug. It's like in* Transformers, *when all those robots get together to make that super-robot. But* way *whinier.*
2. *There's a reason they call it "The Big, Noisy, Drafty Apple."*

ALL THESE PEOPLE HAVE SOMEWHERE VERY IMPORTANT TO GO.

HUGE, SOMETIMES-OPEN STAIRWELLS RIGHT IN THE MIDDLE OF THE DAMN SIDEWALK

Wait a second. Hold up, New York. You want to put huge, sometimes-open stairwells *where?* *Right in the middle of the damn sidewalk?* That's where pedestrians go, New York. How are you going to make sure people don't fall into those huge stairwells when they're walking? Oh. Sometimes, you'll put out a little orange cone? Okay, cool. As long as you're looking out for everybody's best interests. . . .

PROS: It's an efficient way for businesses to load and unload goods from trucks on the street.

CONS: It's an efficient way to fall into a huge effing hole right in the middle of the damn sidewalk.

CONCLUSION: That's a lot of faith to put in one little orange cone.

"LITTLE HELP?" ASKS THE MAN WHO HAS FALLEN DOWN THIS OMINOUS STREET HOLE.
NO HELP WILL COME.

UNION SQUARE

One of the first things you'll notice upon arriving in Union Square is the bronze statue of George Washington, one of our nation's first presidents, atop a majestic steed, with his right arm extended and his right hand open as if he's trying to use the Force to summon his lightsaber and kill an approaching snow beast. The horse, which we've nicknamed Ol' Bronzie, has a lowered head, perhaps to ponder the fascinating history of his surroundings. . . .

In 1815, the city commissioners decided the strangely shaped lot didn't lend itself to commercial development, so they declared it a public commons. It was named by Samuel Ruggles, a local lawyer and politician, who purchased the adjoining lots and expanded the park in order to allow fruit hucksters to sell their wares 150 years in the future.

"I *predicteth* a grand *spaceth* for a farmer's *marketeth*," Muggles [sic] declared in his old-fashioned New York accent or whatever.

By 1845, with Fuggles's [sic] continued encouragement, Union Square was surrounded by houses, trees, and sidewalks. A dog park was added so poodles could sniff each other's poodle-parts and ultimately generate more poodles.

Then, some things led to some other things, and now there's a Staples, and a Babies "R" Us, and a Petco, and a Barnes & Noble where, if they were alive today, George Washington and Ol' Bronzie could mosey over and pick up a copy of *this very book!* Really makes you think, huh?

> **PROS:** Interesting history.
> **CONS:** History always ends with big-box chain stores.
> **CONCLUSION:** Bleh.

"I CANNOT TELL A LIE," SAYS GEORGE WASHINGTON.
"STAPLERS HAS GREAT DEALS ON PRINTER CARTRIDGES."

NEW YORK NEWSPAPERS

It's a tough time for newspapers, many of whom are being forced to cut staff, tighten budgets, and run boilerplate *Dilbert* comics, which, let's face it, are worse than job loss.[1] Most major cities can barely support one newspaper, let alone two, which was actually the norm half a century ago. But *four* major daily newspapers in one metropolitan region would be *impossible* these days, right?

Wrong! Somehow, through sheer determination (read: stubbornness), New York City is still managing to support four mostly legitimate daily papers, for better or worse: the *New York Times*, the *Wall Street Journal*, the *New York Post*, and the *New York Daily News*.

This—the four papers—is a hard feat to accomplish, and we would like to offer New York a variety of pats and rubs and gentle kisses on its back and tummy and earlobe, respectively, for its support of the newspaper industry. Not a sexual thing. Just our way of saying, "Way to go, Inky City! You did it! You really did it, New York, and now we're going to give you the tiniest, softest kisses on your earlobes and collarbone." Nothing weird about that, except that now we've got ink all over our hands.

On the other hand, have you seen the Internet lately? All that shit's free!

> **PROS:** Lotsa newspapers.
> **CONS:** But for how long?
> **CONCLUSION:** Unfortunately, you can't reblog a news item if no one reports it in the first place.

---

1. *Today's hilarious punch line: "And that's exactly why we never get anything done around here." Today's hilarious setup: "I see you're already using the conference room, but I'm going to have a meeting here too." We'll let you guess the hilarious middle panel.*

If you look very carefully, these newspapers have a hidden message.

NEW YORK PUBLIC LIBRARY

Poet Archibald MacLeish once said, "What is more important in a library than anything else—than everything else—is the fact that it exists."

Well, nobody can argue that the New York Public Library doesn't exist. Try: You'd be all like, "That library isn't even *there*." And then your pretty friend Meagan would be like, "Then where did the beginning of *Ghostbusters* take place?" And then you'd stand there in silence for what feels like hours, trying to think of something clever to say. *God, Meagan's so smart,* you'd think. *She's so cool and smart and funny. If only I could come up with some super-hilarious answer that somehow relates to* Ghostbusters *and libraries and maybe it's a little bit flirty, but not too forward . . . we'd be laughing together and having a great time and maybe someday in the future, if someone mentions* Ghostbusters, *she'll think of me and the super-hilarious joke I came up with so quickly. . . .* Three days later, while sitting in traffic, you'd think of the perfect answer, but by then it wouldn't matter. Such is life.

Anyway! The New York Public Library exists, in a *major* way. It's one of the biggest libraries in the world, sporting eighty-eight miles of bookshelves (which, incidentally, makes Strand Books's eighteen miles of books seem like negative-seventy miles of books.)

Unfortunately, if you're looking for a library that does more than *exist*, this one might not be your jam. Yes, it's got beautiful architecture, with columns and carved ceilings and marble lions guarding the entrance, but it's also a "no-browsing" facility, which means that almost all the books are stored underground, and you have to type in the title that you're looking for on one of their computers and they'll get it for you with a mysterious system of dumbwaiters and subterranean mole-people who fetch the books while quietly plotting a bloody uprising.

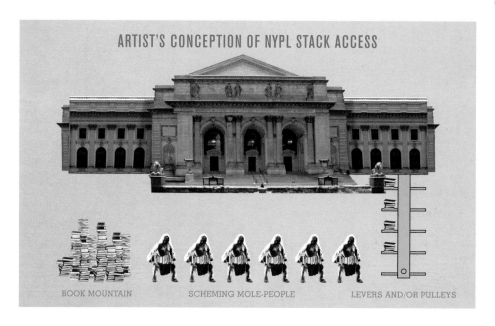

ARTIST'S CONCEPTION OF NYPL STACK ACCESS

BOOK MOUNTAIN   SCHEMING MOLE-PEOPLE   LEVERS AND/OR PULLEYS

We don't want to sound nitpicky, but doesn't that sort of defeat the purpose of a library? The ability to wander around and find books that you weren't necessarily looking for and physically leaf through them with your physical hands? Without books to root through, the New York Public Library is just another big, pretty, sort-of-drafty building that, well, exists.

> **PROS:** Literacy rules.
> **CONS:** It seems like more people are interested in seeing where Carrie got married in the *Sex and the City* movie than finding reading materials.
> **CONCLUSION:** Try one of the smaller branches in Brooklyn or wherever. Fewer tourists, same great books.

FASHION WEEK

Twice a year, New York hosts Fashion Week, when all the biggest designers get together in a massive tent to tell everybody what's totally hot and what is *totally* not. And if all the world's a tent, as Shakespeare wrote, and all the designers and customers are merely players, then it only makes sense that we'd write a one-act play about the ordeal, perfect for your local community theater or dumpy performance space. Standard royalty rates apply.

Fashion Week: A Play in One Act
By Avery Monsen and Jory John

Big Designers: Hey! You there! With the pants! Those pants are not hot!

You: But I just bought these this morning! From you!

Big Designers: Our decisions are totally arbitrary and totally final! NO LONGER HOT!

(You go home and cry.)

Big Designers: Crying is also not hot.

(Curtain.)

> **PROS:** Pretty people. Pretty outfits.
> **CONS:** The whole thing is strategically designed to make you feel like a fat piece of shit.
> **CONCLUSION:** *Auf Wiedersehen.*

CREATE YOUR OWN SIGNATURE STYLE

Coat woven from
shredded tires

$3,200

Cloud hat made out
of goose dander

$9,000

Underwear with a
video screen that
automatically syncs
with your Netflix queue.
**CURRENTLY UNAVAILABLE
TO THE PUBLIC.**

Pants made of live mice

$8,000

Boots made of actual
chimneys

$12,000

I ☺ NY

*I Feel Relatively Neutral
About New York* shirt
(neutralnewyork.com)

$20

GREENWICH VILLAGE

Do you know the album *The Freewheelin' Bob Dylan*? On the cover is a picture of a twenty-one-year-old Dylan with his then-girlfriend, strolling arm in arm through Greenwich Village in 1963. If you have the album, queue up the song "Bob Dylan's Dream" for the remainder of this page. Various keywords in the next few paragraphs will sync up perfectly with certain moments in the song. It'll be like watching *The Wizard of Oz* while listening to *Dark Side of the Moon*.

Anyway, the song just seems to sum up everything about hope, and youth, and closet-size apartments where friends come over and hang out, and you have a few drinks and laugh, and everything is, for the most part, swell. Sure, later on there'll be the the awkward 3 A.M. conversation when you try to decide if your buddy is too drunk to make it home on his own. You'll feel guilty if he gets hurt, of course, but at the same time, your studio is tiny, and you're a light sleeper, and you'd really rather not listen to somebody snore or cough all damn night.

But back to the album: Dylan's pictured on the cover, walking through the Village, and if you go there today, you can sense that some seriously neat stuff happened there. Maya Angelou and Jack Kerouac and Allen Ginsberg were around, doing their things, and you can almost physically feel it. It's pretty great.

At the same time, the Village *these days* is mostly just a bunch of American Apparels and Starbuckses. And there are these NO STANDING and NO HONKING signs, even though standing around and honking is sort of what made Bob Dylan famous in the first place.

PROS: Bob Dylan once walked these streets.
CONS: He's gotten a better apartment, probably, since then.
CONCLUSION: If only we could've been here forty years ago.

THE NEW YORKER

Full disclosure: We both subscribe. What can we say? It's a good magazine, okay? It's funny and interesting and, if you actually live in New York, it'll tell you all the important cultural stuff you should see and do, if you happen to be interested in important cultural stuff.

And if you don't live in the Big Apple, the *New Yorker* offers cultural events that you can enjoy at home, inside your own head, through the magic of reading! That's right, week after week, you can dive into a droll David Sedaris romp or have your brain rearranged by a counterintuitive think-piece from Malcolm Gladwell. It's like having a really great conversation with some well-spoken friends, except none of them give a shit about what you have to say. Delightful!

Fuller disclosure: Sometimes we just skip to the "Shouts and Murmurs" section, read all the comics, and call it a day. Then we leave the magazine on the coffee table to sit and marinate in its brainy juices, in hopes that someone will see it and think we're smarter than we actually are. They'll see that easily identifiable logo-type on the cover and know exactly what they're dealing with, here: brains, class, and panache.

PROS: Insightful essays, sharp satire, fictitious fiction.
CONS: The pile of unread issues is stressing us out.
CONCLUSION: If they offered a half-price, just-for-show coffee table edition that was just a cover and a hundred blank pages, honestly, we'd probably buy that instead.

CHOOSE YOUR OWN "HILARIOUS" *NEW YORKER* CAPTION

1 "Excuse me, sir. There's a fly in my soup, and he's wearing a bowtie."

2 "Does anyone know how long I've been in this restaurant? It feels like years. Where are all the clocks? Who are you? WHO AM I?"

3 "Dinner was fantastic, but the company *stinks*!"

4 "Excuse me, sir. I think there's a small salamander in my wine goblet."

5 "I'm from the future."

SNOW

Nothing quite compares to the twinkle of snow falling under New York street lamps at twilight.[1] It's a gentle reminder that, even in the heart of the big city, there's always the possibility of something fresh and pure and beautiful. You'll honestly feel like you're walking around in your very own romantic comedy and that, despite your gender and sexual preference, John Cusack is definitely about to sweep you off your feet.

On the other hand, in a few hours, all that snow is going to turn into dirty, nasty slush, which is way deeper than it looks, and will inevitably soak through your shoes and socks.

Snow is a lot like Jodie Sweetin, in that respect. One second, she's playing adorable little Stephanie Tanner on television's *Full House*. Next thing you know, she's addicted to meth.

Yes, snow is sort of like that.

> **PROS:** Natural beauty.
> **CONS:** The moment you get home and you take off your shoes and socks, you realize the bottoms of your pant legs are all wet and freezing, and you just want to cry.
> **CONCLUSION:** Bring your galoshes?

---

1. For a nice visual, consult your handy Thomas Kinkade "Painter of Light" daily calendar.

SNOW: A CHRONOLOGY

FRESHLY FALLEN

Oh, magic! Oh, sweet wonder!

FIVE MINUTES LATER

This is the absolute worst.

SEX AND THE CITY

First of all, let it be said that neither of us has ever seen an episode of this show. Undaunted, we bought some tickets for the *Sex and the City* Hotspots Tour.

After boarding the bus at the corner of 5th Avenue at 59th Street, we walked down the aisle, hoping that we wouldn't be the only men in attendance. There was, thankfully, a gentleman sitting near the back. We exchanged silent, knowing looks. "We're only here as a goof!" we tried to indicate. "Don't worry, boys. We're in this thing together," his eyes reassured.

It turned out that he was the driver, and we were the only unpaid dudes in a bus full of moms, most of them seemingly tipsy from midmorning Cosmos. In theory, this is awesome. In practice, we've never felt so alone. As we took our seats, the tour guide announced over the mic that we'd have to fill in for Mr. Big today. We didn't know what that meant—we still don't—but the oversexed mom-giggles that echoed through that bus have haunted us ever since.

The tour took us to *Sex and the City* locations all over Manhattan. Obviously, a lot of it was lost on us, but we tried to join in. We *ooohed* at a boutique where someone named Charlotte bought shoes. We *aaahed* at a boutique where someone named Miranda bought more shoes. We forced laughter at a video clip of Carrie making a lot of terrible, self-satisfied puns.

Mostly we were just very happy to have a nice, clean, warm place to sit for a few hours. Sometimes, in New York, a little thing like that can really make your day.

PROS: The bus was very comfortable.
CONS: All the moms laughed at us.
CONCLUSION: Maybe we'll watch season one and see how things go.

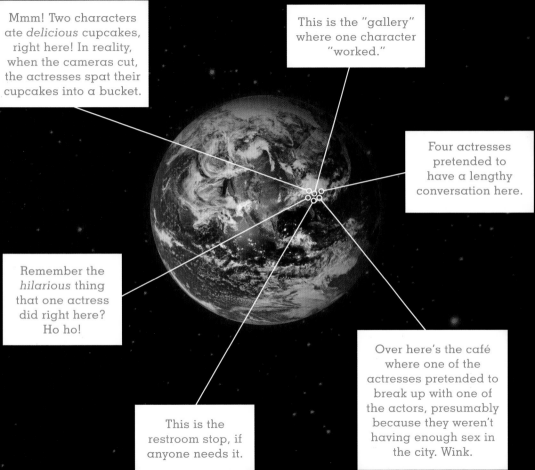

WALL STREET

Q. What's that guy screaming about?
A. Stocks!

Q. Why's that lady in the pantsuit chain-smoking?
A. She's stressed!

Q. What was that collective groan just now?
A. A billionaire just sneezed and sent the market tumbling!

Q. Who works here?
A. Guys who look like the main villain in *The Karate Kid*!

Q. How does it all work?
A. Magic!

> **PROS:** Wealth, as far as the eye can see!
> **CONS:** None of it is real!
> **CONCLUSION:** We'll put our money in a nice safety-deposit box, thank you very much.

CAN YOU FIND ALL THE HIDDEN STACKS OF CASH?

Some silly hedge fund manager has taken all of your cash and hidden it around this Wall Street statue! Can you find it all? Either way, you can't have it back. Sorry!

UNITED NATIONS

Since its inception in 1945, the UN has been committed to improving human rights, fostering communication between nations, enforcing international law, and creating world peace. At least, that's what it said on the bookmark we stole from the gift shop.

And, honestly, we wanted to enjoy the UN. We really did. We're the last guys to bash diplomacy. But they were trying to charge us sixteen dollars for a tour! Each! Who are we, Bill and Melinda Gates? "WE'RE NOT MADE OF MONEY, BAN KI-MOON!!," we hollered. We're pretty sure that, wherever he was, UN Secretary General Ban Ki-Moon heard us, somehow. That's one of his Moon-powers: super-hearing.

So we didn't go on the tour, per se, but we're fine with that, because we decided to create a tour of our own, which was shorter, cheaper, and took place entirely in the UN café. Here are our findings:

1. They didn't accept debit or credit cards. That's right, at the time of our visit, the UN café was cash only. Isn't swiping a Visa card a lot easier than converting rupees to dollars, or convincing some brutal dictator to take a day off, or whatever? On the other hand, maybe they're trying to teach debtor nations (i.e.: us) not to over-rely on credit. If so, mission accomplished.[1]

2. The guy working behind the counter didn't say "Have a nice day" to us until after we said "Have a nice day" to him. Look, this is basic customer service, people! You'd think that to work at the United Nations your minimum job requirement would be to say "Have a nice day" to everyone. Who knows what

---

1. We just Googled it and it looks like they've finally started taking plastic. Debtors, rejoice!

SIDEBAR: A THING WE ATE!

This is a photograph of a muffin that we purchased in the café of the United Nations. It was a little dry, but we ate it because we were hungry, and we are not picky.

This is proof that we will eat most things. This picture was taken after the second bite, but rest assured: We finished that muffin. Thanks, UN café!

kind of ambassadors and dignitaries you're going to be serving in there? Like we've always said: World peace begins in the café.

3. There's no way of knowing for sure, but we're relatively sure the guy restocking the pastries was Boutros Boutros-Ghali.

> **PROS:** Probably doing great work; facilities seem top-notch from the lobby.
> **CONS:** What's with the *charging* for everything? Can't the poor experience unity too?
> **CONCLUSION:** Room for improvement.

NEW YORK BAGELS

Everyone's got at least one friend who just *loves* New York bagels. He can't stand any other bagels. Won't touch them. Any time anybody's eating another state's bagel, he launches into his trademarked NY Bagel Supremacy Rant.

"If there were an Olympics for bagels," he says, "New York bagels would win gold every time. They'd win at the bagel luge, and the bagel curling, and the bagel rhythmic gymnastics, with little gymnastics-ribbon-wands sticking out of their doughy little bagel holes!" And there's this really weird glimmer in his eye when he says "bagel holes" that makes you wonder if he might have, at some point, attempted human-bagel relations.

The point is: When people told us New York's got the best bagels, we were a little skeptical. So we went to all the places that everyone recommended in New York: Ess-a-Bagel, H&H Bagels, Bagel Hole, and a bevy of other bagelries. And they were all good! We never had a bad bagel in New York.

But, then again, neither of us could recall ever having a really bad bagel, anywhere, ever. We both just really like bagels. They're cheap, and you can put all kinds of stuff on them, and eat them with one hand while walking, without even paying attention! So, yes, New York's got good bagels. But that's like saying one particular ATM gives out the best twenties. Everybody loves twenties, okay? Some twenties may be older, foldier, or chewier, but they'll get the job done, and we're happy to have them around.

PROS: Delicious.
CONS: Just tone down the hubris a little.
CONCLUSION: In 2009, and this is totally true, the best-selling bagels in America—with more than half of the market share—were made by Bimbo Bakeries, whose parent company, Grupo Bimbo, is based in *Mexico*.

CAN YOU MATCH EACH BAGEL WITH ITS PLACE OF ORIGIN?

1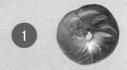

2

3

4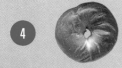

5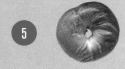

A NEW YORK CITY

B BOSTON

C SAN FRANCISCO

D SEATTLE

E GUAM

ANSWER: NO. NO, YOU CAN'T.

CHINATOWN

To capture our ambivalence about Chinatown, we decided to create a brand-new *hilarious* parody song, sung to the tune of Petula Clark's "Downtown." Look out, Weird Al. We're coming for your job and your wife, in that order.

"My wife?" you say? Yes. Your wife too, Al. Weird Wife Yankovic is coming with us. Get this straight: There are two new comedy songsters in the comedy-song-racket and we're both getting "Weird" legally placed in front of our names. That's how committed we are to this lifestyle. And your career? Well, it's like that one guy said to Jack Nicholson at the end of whatever movie they were in together: "Forget it, Jake. It's Chinatown." (You're Jake, here, Yankovic. Was that clear?)

For sale in Chinatown: inside-out ducks and right-side-out SpongeBobs.

"CHINATOWN" (SUNG TO THE TUNE OF "DOWNTOWN")

Where can you go to find some four-dollar glasses and a SpongeBob shirt?
CHINATOWN!

Where there's wallets and snow globes and some key chains and daggers and
a SpongeBob skirt?
CHINATOWN!

Wander through the streets and you'll be lost within an hour.
Luckily you'll find some tasty chow mein to devour.
How can you lose?

There's so much you can get for a buck!
Just look in that window, there's an inside-out duck! It's in:

CHINATOWN! The sidewalks are crowded in:

CHINATOWN! The mung beans are sprouted in:

CHINATOWN! Everything's waiting for you!

And by "everything," we mean, "delicious food and an overwhelming array
of inexpensive plastic whatsits that we're not sure anyone needs." Maybe
if they were slightly more expensive and less disposable it'd be better for
everyone, but really now, who's to blame here? The vendors selling this stuff
or us, standing here with a plastic bag full of sixty-cent dish scrubbers and
bootlegged DVDs of *Steel Magnolias*? We'll just sit down and have some
mu shu pork and think this through. . . .

BROADWAY

Have you ever been around a cat? Like, have you ever really spent a *significant* amount of time watching a cat walk around and meow and throw up on your rug? You have? Okay. Good. Listen to this idea: We're going to find, like, thirty people—full grown adults, okay?—who are going to put on unitards and face paint and sing and prance around for, like, an hour and a half, pretending to be cats! And people will pay seventy dollars apiece to see it. Or more! Never less. Mostly, more.

Hmm.

To be fair, there are other shows on Broadway that don't feature people dressed up as singing cats.[1] *The Lion King* has people dressed up as all sorts of other singing animals! Including singing lions. Which are totally different from singing cats!

    PROS: Raw emotion. Showmanship. Unitards.
    CONS: The stench of lost dignity and catnip.
    CONCLUSION: Meeouch?

---

1. *Okay, we understand that* Cats *closed in 2000, but doesn't it feel like it's still playing? Like maybe we're all Jellicle cats?*

CATS VS. HUMANS: A COMPARATIVE ANALYSIS

CATS

Cute

HUMANS

Generally pretty good

CATS DRESSED AS HUMANS

Super cute

HUMANS DRESSED AS CATS

Sad and sort of disturbing

"THE CITY THAT NEVER SLEEPS"

Never, New York? Not ever? Really?

Hmm.

Wait, are you sure? You're saying you never, ever sleep?

That just seems like a crazy thing to say. We don't want to beat a dead horse, here, but you're saying you never sleep, you've never slept, and you never *will* sleep? That's what you're saying?

Like, not even when you're really, really tired? Or when you've got something important to do the next day and you want to make sure you're on the ball and looking fresh?

Okay, what about after a big meal? You're telling us with a straight face that you don't get sleepy after a big ol' turkey din-din? No? Well, that just seems bonkers, to be honest. It seems like we exist in two totally different realities. Because in this reality over here—in this non-bonkers reality over here—first you have turkey-time, then you have nappy-time. It's a whole . . . *thing*.

So you never sleep, huh?

Well, it sounds like *somebody's* going to be a *cwanky* city in the *mowning*.

    PROS: There's always something to do.
    CONS: It's always happening right outside your window.
    CONCLUSION: Just drink some warm milk and take a nap, New York.
    You don't have to prove anything to us.

SOMETIMES, SLEEPING CAN BE REALLY NICE.
JUST LOOK AT THIS ADORABLE PUPPY. HIS NAME IS CHAMP.

CONCLUSION

Well, look at you, Sporto! You made it. You've read our entire book, from cover to cover. You sat down and promptly disregarded all prior commitments because you literally could not stop turning these pages. Weeks have passed. Seasons have changed. Boyz have become men. Look in the mirror. That beard wasn't there when you started. (It looks great, by the way. You look like Gandalf's cool, younger brother. Or Dumbledore's hot, bearded sister. Depending.)

So what conclusions can we draw about New York? Well, we've done the math and punched the numbers and accounted for all of New York's various sights and sounds and smells, and it turns out the Big Apple is . . . wait for it . . . here it comes . . .

PRETTY OKAY, OR WHATEVER!

There's lots of good stuff in New York, sure. There are things that you honestly can't get anywhere else. That view from the top of the Empire State Building, for instance. Or the smell of Central Park in late October. Or the feeling that the city itself is somehow alive and pulling you in a hundred directions at once, rife with possibility. No matter how we try, we just can't take that stuff away from New York. Of course, there's plenty of stuff that you can definitely skip, or maybe just watch in a YouTube video, or buy in postcard form. Like, we wouldn't touch the actual Statue of Liberty with a stick. You know how many germs are on that beast? So many germs! A postcard, on the other hand, is relatively clean and makes Lady Liberty look lovely and quite liberty-filled. So that's the take away: Some things good, other things, maybe not so good.

Also, we should probably take this opportunity to apologize to the people of New York: We're sorry, people of New York. We didn't mean to hurt you with our poorly researched, half-assed critiques of your city. To anyone that we've offended: We offer you this metaphorical, but totally sincere, olive branch, free of charge (with price of book plus tax).

To anyone that's still offended even after we've apologized: We take back our apology. You're too sensitive, and you're being sort of a dick about it. Go sit on a New York bagel.

Well, we've done it again. Jeesh. We should probably just end this and move on to something else before we get into any more hot water. For the record, though, after month upon month of writing this book, after thinking about New York, talking about it, and generally living it . . . we would like to state definitively, for the record, with or without your consensus or approval: We're still relatively neutral.

End of story and, coincidentally enough, end of book.[1]

1. *Except for the appendix and stuff.*

APPENDIX

IN THE NAME OF COMPLETENESS AND INCLUSIVITY, SOME OTHER NEW YORK–RELATED THINGS WE FEEL RELATIVELY NEUTRAL ABOUT:

1. Boroughs: Manhattan, Brooklyn, Queens, the Bronx, and any other boroughs we might have missed

2. Mayors: Koch, Dinkins, Giuliani, Bloomberg, Dinkles, Binkles, Broomberg, and McCheese

3. Sports teams: the Knicks, Mets, Yankees, Rangers, Jets, Giants, Liberty, and sports in general, in which we were frequently picked last

4. Buildings: the Woolworth Building, Seagram Building, MetLife Building, Flatiron Building, Trump Building, Trump Tower, Trump Castle, Trump Apartments, Trump Duplex, Trump Sidewalk, Trump Moat, and Trumpland

5. Bridges: Brooklyn Bridge, Manhattan Bridge, Williamsburg Bridge, and most other bridges, including Beau, but excluding Jeff, who has done great work in recent years

6. Celebrities: Spike Lee, Woody Allen, David Letterman, Robert DeNiro, Al Pacino, Kareem Abdul-Jabbar, Danny Aiello, James Caan, Neil Diamond, Richard Dreyfus, Jerry Seinfeld, and Howard Stern

7. New York Botanical Gardens, rooftop gardens, gardens in general, people who talk about gardens, nature, and people who talk about nature

8. New Jersey, because of its proximity, pollution, and reputation

9. *Dick Clark's New Year's Rockin' Eve*, *Ryan Seacrest's New Year's Rockin' Eve*, anything else related to Ryan Seacrest or New Year's, which is almost always a letdown

10. Bjork (because her name rhymes with "York")

11. New York Movies: *New York Minute*, *Maid in Manhattan*, *I Now Pronounce You Chuck and Larry*, *Night at the Museum*, *Analyze That*

12. New York–based TV shows: *Friends*, *Dateline*, *Ugly Betty*, *Gossip Girl*, *N.Y.P.D.* anything, *The View*, *The Today Show*, *Late Night With Jimmy Fallon*, *As the World Turns*, and *Law & Order*

13. The "I ♥ New York" logo

14. Other cities, towns, and villages in the state of New York, including Afton, Akron, Albion, Alexander, Alfred, Amboy, Amity, Bath, Bedford, Beekman, Berne, Canaan, Candor, Catskills, Chester, Clayton, Clyde, Decatur, Dunkirk, East Bloomfield, Elmira, Evans, Fabius, Fishkill, Fulton, Fultonville, Galway, Gates, Genoa, Hamilton, Homer, Ithaca, Jewett, Knox, Lake Success, Le Ray, Le Roy, Macomb, Manheim, Niagara, Nyack, Oakfield, Olive, Oxford, Oyster Bay Cove Parish, Pawling, Pelham, Queensbury, Quogue, Ramapo, Red Hook, Richburg, Sag Harbor, Sanford, Scio, Sharon, Throop, Tioga, Tyrone, Ulster, Utica, Valatie, Victor, Waddington, Waterloo, Worth, Xonkers, Yonkers, and Zew York

15. Listen: We're just two guys. Was there something really important that we should have talked about? Probably. Don't worry, though. The hate-mail form is just a few pages away.

YORKS THAT ARE NEWER THAN NEW YORK

1. Cape York Peninsula in Australia, named in 1770
2. York, an inland town in Western Australia, settled in 1831
3. York Peppermint Patties, created in 1940
4. Dick York, star of *Bewitched*, born in 1928

THINGS MORE INTERESTING THAN CENTRAL PARK THAT YOU COULD FIT INTO CENTRAL PARK

1. 9 Disneylands
2. 100 scale models of Central Park at 1/100th scale
3. 64,000 humpback whales, each wearing a party hat

NEW YORKERS WHO WANT TO LECTURE YOU

1. A guest lecturer at NYU
2. The guy who boards the subway between the two longest stops and begins with, "I'm sorry to bother you, ladies and gentlemen . . ."
3. A guest lecturer at Columbia University

NOTABLE BROOKLYN WRITERS

1. Jonathan Lethem
2. Jonathan Ames
3. Jonathan Franzen
4. Jonathan Safran Foer
5. Jonathan Livingston Seagull
6. Betty "Jonathan" Smith

MEDIOCRE NEW YORK FILMS FEATURING A LOST BABY, CHILD, OR AUTHOR

1. *Home Alone 2: Lost in New York* (1992)
2. *Baby's Day Out* (1994)
3. A good-bye message that Avery recorded on his iPhone while lost on the subway and fearing the worst (2011)

SIMPLIFIED CONVERSION OF STANDARD U.S. MINUTES (SM) TO NEW YORK MINUTES (NYM), DEPENDING ON THE DAY OF THE WEEK AND THE WEATHER

	SUN	OVERCAST (OR SCATTERED SHOWERS)	HEAVY RAIN	SNOW
MON	NYM = SM × 1.4	NYM = SM ± 3	NYM = SM	NYM = SM ÷ the current age of the President of the United States
TUES	NYM = SM × 1.4	NYM = 4	NYM = SM × the current temperature, Fahrenheit	NYM = SM
WEDS (EXCEPT 2ND WEDS OF EACH MONTH)	NYM = SM × 1.4	NYM = 4 ± 3	NYM = SM ± 3	NYM = SM ± 1.4
2ND WEDS OF EACH MONTH	not applicable	not applicable	mostly inapplicable	not applicable
THURS, FRI, AND SAT	NYM = SM × 1.5 (except for February, when the multiplicand is again 1.4)	NYM = NYM	NYM = SM × sum of alphanumeric conversion of current pet's name	NYM = SM, usually
SUN	NYM = SM × 1.4	NYM = 15% of U.S. GDP	NYM = SM	NYM = SM ± 3

ABOUT THE AUTHORS

AVERY MONSEN is a writer and artist and actor currently living in Queens, New York. Yes, *the* Queens, New York. If you want to know the truth, he's terrified of what'll happen to him once this book comes out. He absolutely can't defend himself in a fistfight, and he doesn't have health insurance.

JORY JOHN is a writer and journalist currently living in San Francisco, California. Yes, *the* San Francisco, California. It's absolutely the safer of the two coasts, if you've just written a book about New York being mediocre. Obviously, Jory's terrified of what'll happen to Avery once this book comes out. Avery is frail and malnourished and cries easily, especially at rom-coms.

As a team, Avery Monsen and Jory John are also the coauthors of *Pirate's Log: A Handbook for Aspiring Swashbucklers* and *All My Friends Are Dead*, both published by Chronicle Books. The first one was a kids' book for kids. The second, a kids' book for grown-ups. Their current book, which you're currently holding, is a grown-up book for nobody, in particular. Hmm.

Both Avery and Jory feel relatively neutral about "About the Authors" pages. This attempt is a first draft.

For more Avery and Jory, visit them online at www.neutralnewyork.com or www.bigstonehead.net.

I FEEL RELATIVELY DISAPPOINTED BY THIS BOOK HATE-MAIL FORM

Dear Avery Monsen and Jory John,

I don't think I've ever been this angry. I'm usually a calm, even-tempered person, but your shitty book about New York has got me so riled up I want to punch kittens. Here's why: (check at least one)

☐ **YOU CLEARLY DON'T KNOW ANYTHING ABOUT NEW YORK.**
Neither of you grew up in New York, and Avery only moved there after the book was written! Who do you think you are? Your lazy Wikipedia-based research is riddled with Wikipedia-based inaccuracies. Maybe your next book should be called *How to Con Publishers Into Paying You to Write About Things You Know Nothing About*. Seems like you're pretty good at that.

☐ **YOUR BOOK ISN'T FUNNY.**
I bought this book because I thought your previous book, *All My Friends Are Dead*, was funny. (I continue to buy it for all my friends as birthday and holiday gifts.) What happened to you since then? Family tragedy? Head injury? Something is seriously less funny about the way you string words together. Why can't you write a book with more than 300 words in it without choking?

☐ **YOUR BOOK IS INCOMPLETE.**
Why wasn't there a page about the Yankees? Or the Mets? Or Brooklyn? Or Queens? Or the Bronx? Or Staten Island? Or Long Island? Or JFK Airport? Or LaGuardia Airport; that place is a nightmare! Or the Flatiron Building? Or Trump Tower? Or Carnegie Deli? Or Carnegie Hall? Or Tamany Hall? Or Tamany Deli, if that exists. Or Michael Bloomberg? Or David Letterman? Or Jerry Seinfeld? Or Woody Allen? Or Spike Lee? Or Marty Scorsese? WHY?!

(continued on reverse)

☐ **I HATE YOUR STUPID NAMES.**
They're barely even names, as far as I'm concerned. Honestly, what's a "Jory"? If you say it five times in a row, it becomes gibberish. And "Avery"? More like a-very bad name that your parents chose.

☐ **I FOUND A TYPO.**
It's on page___. Nice copyediting, assholes. For $20, I could've told you that a period goes inside the quotation marks, or whatever.

☐ **THERE ARE A NUMBER OF THINGS WRONG WITH MY LIFE, BUT, FOR THE TIME BEING, IT'S EASIER TO VENT MY FRUSTRATIONS ON YOU THAN DEAL WITH THEM.**
My son won't talk to me. Any tips?

In conclusion, I hope you both get a rash. If you already have a rash, my hope is that it will worsen or spread to your face, more specifically, to your eyes.

Yours in seething rage,

☐ Mr. ☐ Mrs. ☐ Ms. _____ _____ _____
                        (First)   (Middle initial)   (Last)

Age _____ E-mail _____

I'd like a signed 8×10 photo of the authors for framing. ☐ YES ☐ OKAY

How much did you dislike this book? (Circle 1 to 5 flip-offs.)

THANK YOU FOR YOUR INPUT!